Unveiled Pieces of a Broken Mask

By

Shana Gourdine

UNVEILED PIECES OF A BROKEN MASK

Copyright © 2020 by Shana Gourdine

For information contact :
http://www.theladybehindthemask.com

Publishing Company : JK Publishing House LLC.
Book Interior and Cover Design by Desiree J Philmore

Second Edition : November 2020
10 9 8 7 6 5 4 3 2

This book is a spinning of my first book, *The Masks behind the Mask,* and also a book of the next stage of taking your mask off. In my first book, I was letting you know that we all carry a mask where you may have not been comfortable with your imperfections of who you are behind your mask. In this book, I am here to help you unpack the things we carry and hold on to that can end up destroying your relationships (with friends, associates, family or partner). We are going to take time to rebuild the person that you have hidden from the world because you were not comfortable in your own skin. We are going to get uncomfortable to get comfortable with ourselves regardless to what others think about who you are. This is the time to learn who you are and what makes you happy.

NEED HELP SELF PUBLISHING YOUR BOOK ?

Want to make your dream come true and share your story ?

We are here to help you ! **100 % Satisfaction Guarantee**
All Royalities & Rights yours !

Services :

*Ghost Writing

*Editing (Line, Copy and Full Manuscript)

*Book Formatting (Print & E-book)

*Cover Design

*Book Interior Design

*E-Book Conversion

*ISBN Assignment and more

Contact us for your Consultation Today !

Email us :

Frozeninthemidstoffire@gmail.com

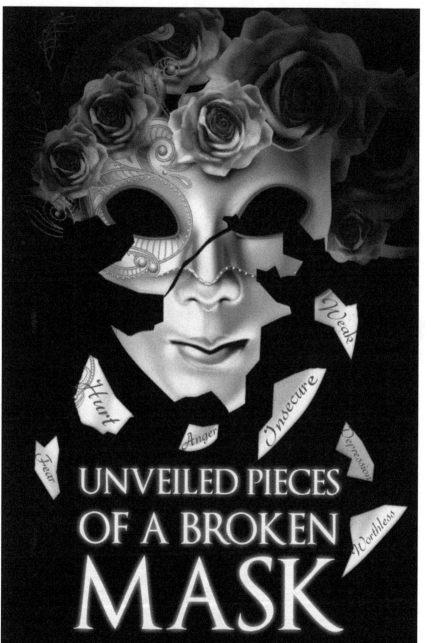

UNVEILED PIECES
OF A BROKEN
MASK

SHANA W. GOURDINE

This book is dedicated to my daughters Leone and Samira Gourdine-Walker who are always telling me that they are proud of me for helping other people heal through my story.

Next, this book is dedicated to my support system that keeps me motivated to continue to tell my story. They showed me that the more dedication you give to your dream, the more it is likely to be a success.

Lastly, this book is to everyone that enjoyed my first book and embraced my poems as if they were your pain too. Thank you everyone for all of your support for last year

and a half.

CONTENTS

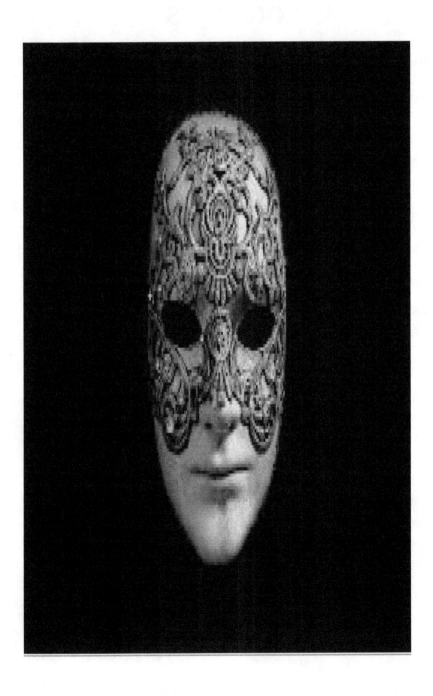

Greetings,

I been asked to include some of my story in my second book. My first encounter of Domestic Violence was in August 2011. I was about seven months pregnant and I got thrown against a cabin in my kitchen and chocked until I finally got his hand from around my neck. I was more worried about my baby's life instead my own. After this occured, I was so shocked, hurt, ashamed, and devasted because as a woman, I could never imagine anyone putting their hands on me. I should have never continued this relationship but like most women, I was blinded by love. It took me a few weeks, because I listened to apologies and The I love you's and honestly, I thought that I could save my family. Unfortunately, I did not press charges. I tried to make it work with my abuser, but in May 2012, it was not long before that demon showed up again. This time I was holding my 4-month-old daughter and my abuser decided to chock me again while I was in my livingroom. I decide that my family was not worth that type pain. Well a few years later, I finally left and got into another relationship. Unfortunately, in 2016, I end up in another toxic relationship. I wondered in my head, what was it that I doing wrong, why do I keep finding myself in relationships with people that have control issues or was dealing with their own trauma from their childhood. This time it was more extreme from my first domestic violence situation. I was dragged upstairs by my hair, I have been chocked in my sleep, called out my name, and had my life threatened of getting my throat slashed. I tried to leave multiple times, and my abuser started stalking me wherever I went. I had to unroot my kids and I to make sure we safely away from a person that wouldn't let me go after it was supposed to be over. I had to get a restraining order and press charges on my abuser because I was tired of fearing for my life all because a person was not mentally stable. It was hard to explain to my young daughters what was happening and that we would be ok in such a toxic experience. I was blaming myself for the horrible trauma that I had brought into our lives.

I started dealing with PTSD, anxiety and depression. As a mother, I felt like a failure, as a woman, I felt destroyed, and as daughter, I felt ashamed. The thoughts of allowing this to happen again was not sitting with me. I had to do something to change the dynamics of my life. I had to figure out what was next for me and my angels. Well this story is to be continued ….

I hope you enjoy reading this book.
Let's begin unveiling the broken pieces of our mask.

Shana W. Gourdine

Insecure

Some people are so insecure that they do not trust anyone around them. Insecure people have some many different problems with relationships because of trust and internal issues.

Sometimes feeling insecure comes from things that we expierenced in our childhoods. Sometimes we are unsure of ourselves and the decisions we have made. In return, we blame others on why things are not going right.

Most of the time our feelings of being insecure comes from low self-esteem, being abuse, being cheated, not loving yourself, and not trusting yourself on feelings we tend to carry around.

We tend to start playing the blame game with others that we are around or associates that we are dealing with in our lives. We blame people for things that we feel about ourselves. We are too afraid to look at ourselves in the mirror. We started accusing people of cheating, flirting, or thinking people are talking about you or feeling some kind of way about you.

In order to work on being secure, you have healed the

things internally dealing with from our past relationships, our childhood trauma, and our own self-images that we have in our mind. We must accept our own imperfections that we have not accepted about yourself.

Internal work takes time. It never happens overnight. You must want to do the work to improve your feelings of being insecure. The feeling of insecurities that you deal with comes from deep

inside of you. You must want better for yourself on some level of growth. When we continue to stay in the same situation or repeat the same pattern, you get the same result. If you do not change the habit or your way of thinking, you will always be in the same state of mind that your trying to get out of.

Insecurities– uncertainty of anxiety oneself, lack of confidence.

Lack of Protection- The state of being open to danger or threat.

We all fit in these categories a few times in our lives. We have been real with ourselves to ask questions about the insecurities we carry around to know what part we played in these factors of the Mask we still carrying around. We have understood that if we want growth and different frame of mind, we must change your thought process.

Just know you hold the power to be better than the person you hide behind that mask.

Mirror Questions for Self-Elevation

How do you deal with your insecurities after you felt less of self-worth?

Do you have any insecurities now?

If so, what are they?

What are you going do to make you insecurities become part of your past?

Baggage

When are you going to let go of your past?

When are you going get rid of the no daddy issues?

When are you going to stop blaming your mommy for your problems?

At times in our lives we attempt to move into adulthood and create a life with happiness and fun. Unfortunately, some of us did not learn the skills to do it on our own. We continue to carry the baggage and add more to the load we were carrying. As we continue, the same cycles you carry such as trust issues, judgement, insecurities, low self - esteem, and abuse are carried into your relationships that you try to build and create with friends, associates, or love ones.

Let start with trust issues, which is number one. You blame your partner for everything from cheating to flirting with your friends and associates because you do not trust anyone. You judge them.

Judgment – you compare your partner to your last few partner because they have similar characteristics to the other individuals that have come and went in your live. You judge them based on your past trauma with low self-esteem. This is where you tend to start doubting yourself, talking negative about yourself, you lack the will to do better, and lack of morals.

Abuse can be physical, mental, verbal, and emotional.

IT'S TIME TO LET THE BAGGAGE GO!!!!!!

No matter time of year, hour of the day, or min of the hour, you must let go of the things that you cannot change. Never feel that you must carry all that heavy weight from your past around. You should never let the negative manifest inside your soul. The longer you let it stay a part of you, it feels like the world is the worst place to be. The longer you sink into the negative of evil emotions, it becomes a part of who you are. It becames so deep rooted your relationship wont work. It will forever be a disruption in your mind, body, and soul.

The baggage is something you have unpacked in order to be a better version of you. You have unpacked in order to make room to be happy, to be able to create a better future for yourself. We must heal from all those evil emotions to remove mask that you carry everyday pretending to be happy.

A Mask can only cover so much of the unhappiness, mistreated, and disappointment you experience in your life.

We as people carry so much different emotions inside of the things that we went through as humans. We carry anger, hate, frustration, and disrespect into our future. We are too afraid of getting to the root of the issue to have better future for yourself. Stop the cycle now so you can give yourself and your future a better chance at happiness, joy, and peace. Do not let your past be the reason you are not the best version of you. If you want to unveil your mask that you carry, take the steps to unpack that luggage that been so heavy for so long. It is not going be an easy task because some of our troubles are heavier than others. We all deserve to be happy.

You must open the window and throw out the trash so you can make room for all positive emotions that is coming your way. Let us smile and be great through this transformation because it is going be different emotions through this process, but it is well worth the work. Do not let this trash spill into your little version of you because you did not clean up your mess and just be blessed with less stress.

We wonder why we are so defensive and insecure about the way people look at you, or what they may say to you. We put walls up because of the pain, the hurt, and the disrespect you encountered.

LETS THE WALL DOWN AND LET THE LIGHT SHINE!!!!!!

Now let us do the work, let's dig out the garage of hurt, the love loses, the dad issues, and playing victim. Let us move into a positive cycle and make yourself happy person.

THIS IS TIME TO LET GO OF THE HEAVY BAGGAGE THAT HAS BEEN YOUR BARRIER FOR TOO LONG.

Reflection Questions

How often do you carry your old baggage to your new relationships?

How many times did you forgive yourself before moving on to any other relationship?

When did you bury your baggage before starting something new?

List the Baggage you carry now

-
-
-
-
-
-
-
-
-
-
-

If still carry all that baggage, why do you?

Lady Behind the Mask Tip:

"Let your past Go so you can be Happy!"

In my last book, I told you that we all have to love our imperfections.

Use This Space to Journal your thoughts

_____

_____

_____

_____

_____

_____

_____

_____

_____

_____

_____

RESTORE OF QUEEN

When you told me you love me?

I thought you cared.

I thought you was that man

That was not going to have no fear.

The man that was going to love all

Of the imperfections I had.

The man that was going to

Help repair these scares.

Instead I am her with new open wounds,

New hurt, new angry, that now must

Be repaired over and over again...

Instead you make me rethink things

About myself, you make my walls go

Up again. I do not want anyone close

To my heart, that everyone keeps tearing apart.

Now am working on me again!

I can repair the wall that someone

Came and tour down again. Now it is

Time for me to restore myself, and love no one

Else until my heart is restored without any doubts.

Restore the Queen on her throne

Restore the strength in my soul

Restore the trust and loyalty that people stole

Restore the self -worth of who I am

Restore the crown back to my head

That was tipped by your selfish soul.

I am a person that was hurt

I am a person that has imperfections

I am that person that learned from my lessons

and mistakes.

You came to destroy me, but

I learn to be this fantastic person

That I am today!

I AM STILL STANDING

TOO COMFORTABLE

When you let go of our past

You start breaking your mask.

When you start self-loving

Yourself,

You have start removing your mask

When you stop sitting too comfortably,

You start to release your pieces that you

Been hide behind

We must Let Go!

Start self -loving yourself and get

Out of your comfort zone to

Remove your mask

We get so comfortable in hiding

Behind the mask that it becomes your reality.

At times you do not

Know that the image you pretend

To be is the reality you live.

Give the world the imperfections

Of you because it okay to not be perfect.

Just do not sit too comfortable behind your mask.

Reflection Questions

How comfortable with your life are you right now?

What changes do want to make to your life?

What are the things you value most in your life?

Lady Behind the Mask Tip:

Happiness is within you!!!!!!!

THINK BACK TO HOW YOU USED TO BE AND DESCRIBE WHO YOU ARE NOW. JOURNAL YOUR ANSWER HERE.

_____

_____

_____

_____

_____

_____

_____

_____

_____

_____

_____

_____

_____

_____

_____

_____

_____

_____

_____

_____

REBUILDING OF THE HEART

When you been through a few rough relationships it hard to trust people when you been hurt several times. You try to figure out how to love again. You question things about the person you trying to get to know.

You have so many emotional walls built

up that we doubt and second guess ourselves.

How are you going love again?

We must learn how to allow people to love us again.

We must learn to allow the walls to come down that we put up.

We must learn to work on yourself as you allow others

into our world again

In order to move on you must dump the garage of your past out.

Revaluate yourself on what your worth is.

As you rebuild the inside to be as beautiful

As your outside,

Allow the pretty caterpillar to turn to the beautiful

Butterfly

Allowing your internal instinct to come through and love with no

Judgement.

Love with an unhurt heart, like when you were kid and it was pure

With no expectations was just for a person to love you, respect you,

And to be loyalty to you.

JUST REMEMBER TO REBUILD YOUR HEART TO CLEAR ALL YOUR PAIN AWAY

EMBRACE ME

Today, I introduce the women who went through a tragedy and toxic experience. I have been hurt from my past, cheated on and called out of my name. Yes, I also suffered through mentally, physical, and verbally abuse.

We commonly ask the question "How to do you get back to being yourself after all the hurt, the pain, the disappointment, and the sadness you felt?"

You must find your worth
You must create happiness for yourself
You must love yourself to know you

Have the power within your soul to
Understand your status of who you are
Within yourself

How many times are you going doubt your ability to become a better version of yourself?
Becoming more than what and how people feel about you.
How many times are you going allow your low self-esteem to be a barrier to understand your worth?

Understand the person that is within you
Understand your power of your soul
Understand the ability to use your tragedy,
 your hurt as a story and a scar
to learn who you were made to be

So many times, we allow the past to stop your progression in life. You use it as a clutch to not move on and not let it go!

Many times, we must do some soul searching to look at our own flaws and imperfections. Learn to accept who we are and try not to fit into society because it seems cool. Many times, it hard to except the true of who we are behind the mask. Many times, you need to just forget the judgement, except that we not perfect, and we cannot be a machine and be what everyone else wants us to be.

Right now, I am introducing you to a woman that create my own lane to motivate myself and others to Love Yourself More.

I have rebuilt myself into a Phenomenal Woman of love, happiness and self-worth.

Stop waiting on someone to give you happiness.
Stop waiting on someone to give you love.
Stop waiting on someone to give you a life that means something.

UNVEILED PIECES OF A BROKEN MASK

You must master your life for yourself then everything will fall in place

Always remember that
You are Amazing
You are beautiful
You are phenomenal
You are truly a Queen
Remember you had your power and the glory.

DELIGHT

My soul is delighted to embrace the
Alpha Man that you are
My heart is delighted to embrace the
Big heart that you have that
You do not allow everyone to see
My body is delighted to embrace the
Journey that you take me on
Every time your inside of me
My mind is delighted to embrace the
Conversations we have when we are
having when we spend time with eachother.
My soul is delighted to embrace the
Love connection that we have between us.
The amazing smile, love, and joy that
You have embarked on me is amazing.
The first time having a conversation with you, I
Never knew that our love would grow and you would be
the man, of my dreams, man of my heart, and the man
of my world.
I am delighted to embrace you as my peace, joy, my heart,
And absolutely my soul

FEELING ME SOFTLY

As you lay me down and caress my thighs
And lick my neck, you make my chocolate
Drip so wet.

As you kiss between my legs and make
My body warm and slippery wet, you make
Every moment as a memory I do not want
To forget

As you press against me and I feel
Your manhood begins to operate
I know my skin making you evaluate.

As you continue to caress me up and
Down my body,
You make my body
 Leak like a broken faucet.

Now as you open my legs and
Enter inside my body, I continue
To explode.
The more you stroke, the more
My body leaks, my juices splash
 all over you.
The pleasure is so intense that I cry for you to
Stroke me more and more because
I do not want it to stop.
Hard and slower, slower and harder it goes

Daddy, I just want you to please me
More and more till the sheets are
Soaking wet

Lick me, kiss me, please me

Harder and slower
Slower and harder
It goes
As I open my eyes, I notices
It was just my imagine of you
When you make love to my soul
Not just my body.

NOT ANYMORE

From a Woman who has overcame the tragedy of my life. The hands of other people that want me to fail. Yes, I was abused by a person who was consume of their own selfish ways. yes, I was abused by a self-centered and power tripping personality. He wants me to be powerless and depended on his validation. He wanted me to not like myself because he did not like who he was as human being. He was insuring, with his own trust issues, and still stuck in his control and possessive ways. He still dealing with his childhood trauma and tragedy and blame me for his problems. As woman who found my worth, I was motivated to better as women, as Mother, as friend, and as human being.

TODAY WAS THE LAST TIME I WILL BE CONTROLLED.
TODAY WAS THE LAST TIME I WILL ALLOW YOUR
SELFISHNESS TO AFFECT ME

The moment you felt that I was beneath you was moment you chose the wrong person

I WILL NO LONGER STAND TO BE DISRESPECTED BY YOUR CONCEDING BEHAVIOR
I WILL NO LONGER STAND TO BE BELITTLED BY YOUR CROWDLY BEHAVIORS

THE MOMENT YOU LEARN AND FEEL YOUR POWER YOU WILL STAND YOUR GROUND FOR YOUR SELF-WORTH

I regained my self-worth, learned to love myself and got back my power when I found out the power and knowledge of the Queen, I am

Queen, you need stand proud of the throne you are destined for, stand up to be the strong and take control of your soul.

Positive Quotes

Stand tall with all that you do and keep your faith!!!

My knowledge is my power.

Keep striving for success regardless of the struggle or barriers that may arise

You are the only person that can bring you happiness

Use your scars as your story

There is a light at end of the tunnel

Use your pain as your ambition to go as far as you dream

The Moment

The moment we lock eyes
It was a magical connection.
A connection that was greater than no other

The moment it had us in our first conversation,
my heart was pumping like it was going explode.

But before I allowed my body to take over
I had to learn and understand
Who I was allowing in my peaceful space.

The moment you put your arms on me,
I felt like melting chocolate on a hot summer
Day, even thought it was only a hug, it felt like

A knight and shining armor that took all my problems
Away.

The moments we did not speak or a text did not come
through,
Something starts making me feel different about you
In this moment, I was unsure if its lust or love.
As the time continues with you, it allows me to get to know
you.
My true king that is amazing as he grows in front of me
A man that was looking for his Queen

As these moments continue, we are starting to create a
family between us

The moment I open my eyes and look next me your laying
next me and tell me "Good Morning My Queen". You
treat me as royalty and queen I always was suppose to be.

As this love continue to grow
As this love continue to bloom and get stronger
it makes us become one.

DAYS LIKE THIS

Many days I sat in these
Four walls and cried.
Many days I sat in these
Four walls and felt like
I was not good enough
Many days I sat in these
Four walls and felt sorry
And ashamed of myself.

Now many of us have been in these states of mind because
we did not love who we were
We must have the ability to look at ourselves in the mirror
And motivate ourselves to know we are worth the most
Highest form of love that we deserve
You must believe that your royalty
And should be treated like a king/queen
Nothing less than that
Know that you carry the strength to be greater
and knowledge to be better than before
Know that you are powerful than what society make it
Look like.
You do not have to be a product of your environment

Know that you have taken the time to realize
Who you are, and what you stand for.

IF YOU STAND FOR NOTHING,
YOU WILL FALL FOR EVERYTHING

Keep motivating, inspiring, and empowering your soul.
Keep your head up and continue this journey to be great

LOOK INSIDE

You're always yelling "I'm not worried about nobody. I only
Worry about myself"
Well today, let us do a mental checking,
"When was the last time you sat and
Worked on yourself?"
When was the Last time you talk about your flaws?
Today, I remember being loveable and happy
When I allow others into my peace for space. How could
I allow people?
To disrespect me. How could I allow you to make me
feel lower than my sel-worth?
I started allowing my self-worth to be lower and put
down because I did not love me for me
We step into relationships with all this baggage that
we have not cleaned out yet and we expect
It works without taking care of the inner self-
healing we need to have before we start
Something new.
We need take time to take care for ourselves and stop
feeling as if we cannot be alone
Not be able be alone and love us we be a down fall because
we not taking the time to
Take the time to learn ourselves and not rely on others for
our happiness.
Our happiness is our job not anyone else's.

Journal your thoughts

_____

_____

_____

_____

_____

_____

_____

_____

_____

_____

_____

LIFE STRUGGLES

When life tries to fight you
You have to be ready to fight back.
You have to be ready to
Stand your ground
And be able to withstand
The blows that you are going to receive
Unfortunately, life is not all Peaches and cream.
We learn that there
are people that do not
Want to see you rise.
They rather see
You fall and be defeated.
The strength that you
carry is knowledge.
Your knowledge Is power.
Be great in all you do.
Never let anyone
Tell you any different.

MANY NIGHTS

Many Nights I dream of your amazing soul
Many Night I dream of my ambitions and goals
Many Night I dream of our future and memories
We will make.

I dream of the house and car.
I dream of the children we will going make.
I dream of how our future is going to be great.

Many nights I am laying across my bed
 imaging you in between my legs
Many nights I just love how you put me to bed

I dream of our love and success
I dream of the glitter and gold
I dream of the way we are going rule the world

Many nights I watch you and I know that
You are the man that makes me whole.
Many nights I wonder what made you
Choose me to be your queen to be
Many nights you reassure me that I am
A beautiful queen and I am more precious than gold
And more amazing then anything in this world
Today I dream of our future as we become one.

Today I smile, knowing your mine.
I have cried knowing I was hurt at one point.

I have now realized what
Makes me strong
We all have fell at rock bottom

We all have allowed, or let our mind be us
Own worst enemy
We all have been lost
Until you find your purpose

TODAY, I RISE TO BE AN AMAZING QUEEN
YES, I'VE HAD MY SHARE OF LOW SELF -ESTEEM,
LACK OF SELF-WORTH, AND NOT KNOWING HOW TO
MAKE MYSELF HAPPY.

At one point in my life, I was dealing
with depression, anxiety, and fear.
I have learned how important self -love is to love your self
I have learned how important self -worth is to have.

We all have fell as if the world is on our shoulders
We all have dealt with life situations
That we did not expect to occur.

Now we learn how to set the boundaries
Now we learn how to empower ourselves
When no one else gives you the praise
Now we have learned the benefit of inspiring
Yourselves along with uplifting someone else

Continue to stand in your purpose
Continue to educate yourself on who
you are and what you stand for

You are beautiful inside and out
You are strong enough to prevail
Through all your goals
Your success lays inside of you.

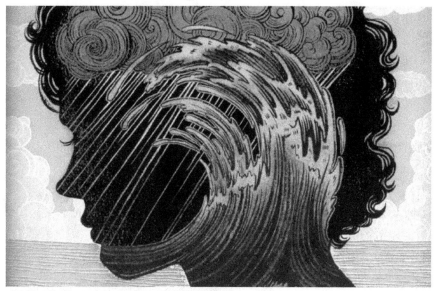

MANY TIMES

So many times, I fear loving anyone again.
So many times, I fear allowing someone next to my fragile heart.
So many times, I did not trust anyone's words because I been lied to, talked about and mistreated.

I have reason to allow people back into my peace.
But the question still stands, "Are they here for your joy or to see you hurt?"
The last time I allowed the same person back into my fragile heart,
They destroyed the little joy and happiness I had.

I often ask myself, "How are you going to be that pure, happy, and joyful person that you used to be?"

The level of rebirth of yourself is not easy. It takes work and strength. It also takes self love and passion.

As many times we say as human beings we want to be a better version of the old you.
One thing you must remember is in order to be
new version, (new birth of yourself) you must bury the
old you. You have an unveil for all those trust issues,
the self-pity, the fear of not being good enough.
Leave your past and never bring up the old you up.

Next step is accepting who you are not who you trying
to be, not who the world wants you to be, not trying to
accept who society want you to be
As you start pouring into who you are
As you started inspiring yourself with positive
You on your journey to a better you

Next, you can move into the stages of the things that brings
you joy.
The things that make you happy should be
Your passion to live for you is everything to live for your
happiness.

The journey will not be easy, you will be tested on your
journey to see if the old you are buried. Always remember
that you got this. Your stronger than you think
you are. You always held the power, it just lost because you
lost it one point in your life.

REMEMBER THE PROCESS ALL STARTS WITH YOU. YOU ARE POWERFUL AND POSITIVE.

Journal your thoughts

_____

_____

_____

_____

_____

_____

_____

_____

_____

_____

Right love

Do you every wonder if you supposed be loved?
Do you every wonder if your deserving of love?
Do you every wonder why they would even love
A person like you?

Its the moment of weakness of your past.
It's the moment of lack of love for yourself.
It's the moment of self-worth of who you are

Never allow the doubts to be the reason why a
relationship does not work
Never allow the doubt of who you are be the reason you do
not allow love to fall apart
You must remember to be strong through your weakest
hour.

After trauma it is thought to receive love from
someone that really love you from the bottom
of their heart.
After so many years of dealing with the man child instead
of real man that supposed to love you and care for you,
the perception is different
After all the name calling, after physical hurt, and
emotional pain, it may be hard but you must delete those
thoughts day by day.

You have allowed the love and the passion to
be genuine and trust the process.

I know your saying "Now Miss Lady Behind Mask, this is going be a struggle!"

To accept love when I do not know what true love is

This is when you have learned what real love is, not the hurt love which was not love in first place.
We should take time for ourselves for
Our hearts to love again
We have learned that we deserve
To be love right by the right person
Yes, we been through a horrible moment
In our life.
Yes, we made through the storm
Use your scars as your story as
You embrace the new beginning
And the new you.

You can trust your judgement again I know it hard, but you got this
No relationship is never easy, but it takes strength, respect and communication
You got this just keep up your process and you can have all happiness you can imagine

JUST LET THEM LOVE YOU THE RIGHT WAY!!!!!!!

Use This Space to Journal your thoughts

_____

_____

_____

_____

_____

_____

_____

_____

_____

_____

It Takes Work

Relationships are a lot of work.
Most of the time it's the conflict in personality differences.
A lot of times, we are so busy trying to be an individual in
our relationships instead a team.
There is no I in team, yes, we are individuals, but we
are supposed to one in relationships.
We represent are partner when we are not together.
Yes, we have all been in the honeymoon stage of
our relationships, that's when things are so lovable
and beautiful.
 Well, sorry be barrier of bad news, but that
phase goes away quicker than you think,
now it is the time to face the real work of staying together.
We all have opinions, we all have beliefs, and we all have
standards.
The problem is when the ego's, trust issues, respect,
and broken hearts can be a damaging key to why the
relationship did not work.
We have to air the trash out and get rid of all of the
negative baggage.

 In order to survive a new relationship, you have come
with an open heart and open mind.
 You cannot come with a clouded mind or judgement about
your past relationships
You must value people on who they are and not who you
are trying to get them to be.

LOVE IS A HARD ROAD. BE READY FOR THE
ROLLERCOASTER! CHERISH EACHOTHER AND WHAT YOUR
WORTH IS!!!!!!

What are you going to do different in your next
relationship?

_____

_____

_____

_____

_____

_____

_____

_____

_____

_____

Feelings

Today I hurt
Today I feel judgement
Today I feel like love hurts

Have you ever gone through a tragedy and worked on rebuilding yourself?
In less than a second,
Someone can put you back to the point of where you use to be.
How can you be who you are, if everything you do is judging someone or making comments on them?
The moment you accuse me of giving my time or attention to someone else that is a damper to my heart.
Do you know how many times I have fought, or felt like I had to prove my actions, trust and loyalty?
I am tired of trying to prove who I am and how true I am to someone.
My mission is to love you for who you are and never try to make you into another person than who you are.
I can only be 100% me, if that does not fix your standards than I may not be that woman you need me to be.

Reflection Questions

How many times have you been hurt and did
not express your feelings?

How do you express that your hurt?

How do you deal with your pain?

ALWAYS LOVE YOURSELF BETTER

As I lay down and close my eyes
I see the smile on your face
As we hug, I feel the
Broken strength of your embrace
As we conversate,
I hear the words of what
The world has filled you
With so much hate.
You have to put yourself back
On your throne,
that no one else can take your
Happiness away.
Reminding you that you
Are strong regardless
Of who maybe giving you fake love
Standing in your truth
Standing in your faith
Knowing your worth is truly a value.
Your inner strength is what grooms you
No matter the faces you see
Remember your brilliant in whoever you may be.
Remember your strength is inside of you.
No one can take it away
Despite the trails you carry
You will survive for another day
Hold your head up high and love
All of what is inside of you

Your heart has healed and
Forgive itself
NOW LOVE YOURSELF TILL THE END

Journal your thoughts

_____

_____

_____

_____

_____

_____

_____

_____

_____

_____

_____

Truth Be Told

People wear mask to cover the many faces
they carry around in society to fit the stereotypes
of an image that is being portrayed.

Many times, people are too afraid of being themselves.
They pretend to be many different versions of people.
Many times, I imagine lying next to a person that I plan on
marrying.

Many times, you imagine that person as the one person
that is going love you, care for you, and respect you.

You see yourself loving them forever and hope
that they will be your partner for life.
Now imagine this person beating you
Imagine this person choking you,
and imagine this person disrespecting you.

How many times have we allowed the love to blind us of
who people really are?
We are so focused on what they are telling us and not on
the action and lack truth that they show us.

Too many times, they may betray you or disrespect you
and you still try see the good in that person.

I have learned through my transformation that I have let go
and stop holding on to people that God is removing out
my life. I have learned that everyone is not meant to go on
my journey.

Many times, we listen to fake apologies, the fake I love you's and accept gifts that present to smooth everything over.

OFF TRACK

Have you ever felt like you were stuck and nothing
was working?
Have you ever thought about your dreams and just
gave up?
Have you ever felt like your loss the ambition to work
towards the things you need to do to reach your dreams?

Let us turns your ambitious back on
Let us get that batteries charged back up
Let get those plans and goals back on track

You might of went off track for a second
You might have lost your drive for second
You might have lost your ambitious for your purpose

YOU WILL GET BACK ON TRACK
NOW LET'S WIN!!!!!!

MANY TIMES, PT.2

Many times, I doubt self
Many times, I did not like
The girl that was looking at me
in the mirror
Countless times I just
Disappointed myself and others
This is the countless effort of not
Pouring into oneself
This is the countless effort of not
Working on your self- esteem
Stop and look in mirror
Learn who you are as a person
Learn your strengths and weaknesses
Learn how to validate yourself,
Do not wait on society or your friends
For confirmation.
Learn about the power you hold
And know that no one can take that away.
Learn the purpose you have for your life
Learn that you have it all inside of you

Yes, at one point in my life I was not sure about who I was.
I was a lost little girl still searching and dealing with
daddy issues, low self-esteem, and trying to still figure
out who I am.
Yes, it was a point in my life where I felt that no one
understood what I was dealing with.
It was days that I couldn't explain the reason I felt that I
wasn't okay.
It was days that I felt that I was ugly
or even worth anyone's love.

During these times, I felt very lonely, depressed, and a lack
of faith in myself.
I have been in some dark places in my life that did
not always feel so great.
I found myself drowning in loneliness and fear
that caused a lack of self-esteem.
We be isolated ourselves from world during these
times because we do not want anyone to judge the things
we are dealing with at that moment.
I decided to take a stand for what our worth is because we
deserve to be respected
We deserve to be loved the right way
We deserve to be happy.

I decide to take a stand and love myself back
I decide to take a stand respect myself
I decide to take stand and trust myself more
Today, I am making a stand for who I am,
the respect I deserve, and the love I require.
Nobody can ever take my peace, joy, and happiness away

I am stronger than I ever been before
I am more powerful than I have ever been before
I am greater than yesterday

YOU NEVER WILL TAKE MY JOY AWAY!!!!!!!

The moment you realize that you
are amazing person and nobody can stop what your
purpose is, you can reach for stars.

You control your destiny for what you want to be in life.
Do not let your struggles hold you back from where you can
be in life.
I know it can be hard or feel like you cannot make it.
Let me tell you that I worked hard at the success I
have encountered.
I took a stand
I'm sure its people that want to see me fail
but I am greater than what society expected out of me.
You have put your ambition on your back,
put power in your soul and
determination in your brain and know that nothing is going
stop that powerful combination.
Use your knowledge for your power.

REMEMBER: IF YOU'RE NOT PUTTING IN THE EFFORT,
YOU CAN ONLY BLAME YOURSELF!!!!!!

I HAVE A TESTIMONY

I HAVE A STORY
I HAVE NOT BEEN PERFERCT
I AM A SURVIVOR
I AM A FIGHTER
MY TESTIMONY IS MY BLESSING
AND I WILL CONTINUE TO BE STRONG UNTIL THE END!

EMBRACE Pt.2

I am embracing the mask that I once hide behind.
I am no longer a prisoner of my past.
I am no longer bonded by my toxic situations.
I am no longer a hazard to myself.
I have reevaluated my life andd change my structure of my
mindset to change the thoughts of my mind.
I have protected my structure of my universe
to protect my peace.
I have learned to love me.

I have embraced my imperfections and understand that I
maybe not be a perfect person.
I have learned that as long as I love myself and
teach me to make myself happy.
I have embraced my flaws and know that
it just takes work to better yourself.
I have embraced the moments of loving me for who I am
So, let us take this journey of loving yourself, embrace all of
your imperfections, and know that it is going be okay when
someone does not embrace you the way you need it to.
You have all tools to make yourself happy and give yourself
love.

EMBRACE YOUR MASK AND EMBRACE YOUR STRENGTH
POSITIVITY IS THE POWER TO TRUE PEACE

WE FIGHT

We are afraid of racism
With no peace
We have face discrimination
With no justice
We have to face violence
With no charge for it.
With these barriers that we face there's
So many obstacles we must overcome
With strength, we can have power
With wisdom, we can gain knowledge
With conversation, we can gain understanding

We can overcome these barriers by the strength we gain.
We face from the world today.

I STAND

Today, I stand in your presence as a woman that was
broken, hurt, and unhappy with myself.
Today, I stand in your presence of shedding my mask that
I use to hold on to because I was afraid of judgement.
Today, I stand in your presence as a woman who went
through the storm and the rain.
Now, I have to let you know the scares of my story,
now let us get to know the woman that is
Standing in front of you.
I am a woman of power
I am a woman of strength
I am a woman of happiness
I am a woman of peace

The strength and power that I have regained.
I will never let anyone to every take my joy away.

The person I have became is a hero
I am a hero that the world knows today
The person I have become will be the woman my children
will look up too as they continue in their lifetime
I cherish this beautiful soul that I have rebuilt
To be a queen and upheld my throne

How are you feeling? Journal your thoughts

_____

_____

_____

_____

_____

_____

_____

_____

_____

_____

Who is the person you are today? Journal your thoughts

_____

_____

_____

_____

_____

_____

_____

_____

_____

_____

BEEN BROKEN

Fixing a broken heart
can sometimes be a hard road to drive on.
When your broken, you tend to want to hurt others
Hurt people tend to hurt other people.
How many times are you going to apologize for the same
thing that you repeatedly say that
you would never do again
Just because you do not hit me
does not mean the verbal and emotional abuse
do not hurt any less.
How many times are you going to tell me you did not mean
to hit me, call me out my name or disrespect me?
When in the same breath, you go and repeatly do it again.
If you slap me, should I turn the other cheek?
If you disrespect me, should I just let go of
what you just did?
Many times, it's a lot harder to realize your worth
after so much pain
How many times have you been told that
you are not worth shit or
Made you feel less than a human being?

I WANT CHANGE

At times we try to not show our emotions
At times we try to remove the pain
At times we try to love again
At times we try to get ourselves together

As we grow into a better person,
we try move on from our past.
We must reconstruct our mind, spirit, and our soul.
We must gather ourselves together and
sit in front of a mirror
And be truthful with ourselves
about how we want to move on.
Allow ourselves to be honest with how we are going make
ourselves a better version of you

In Memory of My Sister

My Angel

The beautifulness of your personality

The grace of your smile.

You were a ray of sunshine, that brightened up this world.

You always had smile on your face and brought joy to my world.

Know we will meet again, on our own stomping ground.

We love you till the end of time. We know you
are watching over us on your spiritual grind.

There is nothing that is going to heal the pain of you not
being here anymore, but we are going to let
your love soar.

In Loving Memory of My Best Friend
Ishia Washington
11-15-19

DAMAGED

As many times as she smiles, she is still hurting inside

As many times as she tries to let it go a new
perspective pop in

As many times as she moves on something in her path
brings her back

It takes her back to the tragedy, the pain and the hate that
she is required to remove from her heart and brain

This beautiful Queen is damaged and abuse

But always she is rebuilding herself on her throne.

Despite the tragedy she has been through, she determined
to be an amazing, uplifting phenomenal,

and inspiring woman the is purpose of who she be.

Did you wake up wanting to be here today?
Did you wake up loving yourself today?
Did you wake up not feeling worthless?

If you answered yes to all of these questions,
this means you are having a great and happy life.
Unfortunately, someone else in the world woke up today
with different feelings.
Unfortunately, someone is dealing with a lack of support,
a lack of self-love, and a lack of faith.
We sometimes are so clouded in our own
drama, feelings, and life situations that we forget to take a
moment
and check on others because we so consumed of our own
struggles.
We have learned how not to be worried so much on things
that we cannot control or the things we can't change.
Have you ever felt any those feelings above?
If you have, then you know that they need an ear
to listen, a shoulder to cry on, and someone to give them
faith and support to let them know that everything is going
be okay.

I have had these thoughts before,

and it did not feel good walking around
with no one to talk to.
I felt alone.
Learn to be a support system for someone!
It may change their lives.

Below are some positive quotes that can help you in your most vulnerable moments

Many times, we are our own worst enemy

Always be the one to empower yourself and embrace your happiness

You are the queen/king of your throne

Focus on your craftmanship and support yourself
with positive energy

Your hustle is your way of life

You are responsible for your own actions

Give yourself a chance to succeed

Love yourself first

I have to value yourself before someone else will value your worth

Trust yourself first before you move into another situation

Use your scars as your story

I have been asked a lot of times
"Why I did write my book?".
To be honest, I wrote poetry to help me through my rough
times.
My rough moments when I felt I was all alone.
My rough times when I feltl no one was listening.
My rough moments when I thought that I was not going to
make it through the storm.
This was worst time of my life.
I was dealing with depression, anxiety, PTSD,
and loneliness.
I felt that I was not worth of anyones time or their love.
Have you ever felt that you were not deserving of love?
Have you ever felt that no one understood your situation?
It's a very dark spot to be in because you
start shutting yourself away from everyone.

I was carrying so much hurt from my past that I did
not know how to love myself.
The pain went so deep that alcohol became my
best friend.
I rather drink than to face the problems I had rolling around
in my head.
I felt so ashamed of the things that happened to me.
I did not want to tell anyone about it because I was
not ready to be judged.
I was not willing to let no one in yet.

It hard to face the world but I realized that it was time to
face the reality. It was time to let people know
and understand that we may feel alone but we are not
alone. I had to become a speaker for people

that couldn't speak.
It felt good to release all of those heavy loads,
and it was necessary.
My poetry gave me an outlet and voice to speak.
Many people use different methods of expression and mine
is poetry.
This was my way of escaping the things that was
not making me feel so good about myself.
It was easier to write down my feelings than to open up to
people that I felt would only judge me.

Many times, we do not really want people to
give advice, we prefer that they just
be geared to listen. A lot of times, we just need support
from someone that not going judge us from our past or
what a person is going through.
I face a lot of hard times during this transformation that
I did not talk about because I choose to encourage
myself through the dark days. When those times came
around, I found the strength in my faith, and myself. I need
you to know that if I can pull myself out of the mud, you
can too.

I TOOK MY POWER BACK!

Transformation Quotes

In order to be a true self, you must unveil mask to be true self

Success is taking hard work and dedication to your crafts

Stand in your truth, loving yourself and your imperfections is the best love and peace you can have

Perfectly imperfect

Sometimes the weight you are carrying around
 is not the weight you need to lose is not your body weight.

You are better than the mask you put on to blend in with society

Look in mirror and learn to love the person you see in front of you

Only way to fail is to not try at all

This was not an easy transformation from overcoming domestic violence and abuse. Understand that domestic violence is not just physical, it's also mental, verbal and emotional abuse, which is all still abuse. It is not just when you get hit by your partner, getting called out your name or being put down to make you feel less than a human being or being talked to like you do not matter. Disrespecting you as you do not average up to them is not OK in any shape or fashion.

In lighter terms, we all have expierenced some problems where we should have acknowledged them. You probably have been with someone that you probably should have left alone because they not treating you right. You may even have had someone that may have tried to control you and make you do what they wanted you to do. You need to learn the signs of an unhealthy relationship and learn to always love yourself first.

So how did I handle my situation?
I went to therapy first to understand myself and understand the reasons why I kept picking the same type people in my life.
A lot of times, when things go wrong, we tend to start blaming others for things.
Yes, they play a major part, but we have to understand what part we played in it too.
No, I am not saying that they were not wrong for what they did.
You just will figure your role in the situation.
We forget that we allow certain characters to be in our lives and let things go on that should not.

As humans, we allow people to still stay because we ignore the signs of the true them. We keep looking the other way because we think it get better.

My next step was learning to love me.
The good, the bad, and the ugly.
I went dates alone, I went concerts on my own and movies on my own.
I taught me about the things I loved and what I liked.
I was able to date yourself and love all of
my imperfections.

Now today, I am still learning to love me, the difference is, I know what I want in my peaceful space.
I know that I bring my own happiness to my life, and I won't take any love that is less than I deserve.

 So, if you feeling that you are going through this
process by yourself, know that you are not alone. We will go through this journey of healing together.
Stay positive and know that you got this!

Journal your thoughts

_____

_____

_____

_____

_____

_____

_____

_____

_____

_____

TONIGHT

Laying me down and making me feel your body
press against mine
Making me moan as I start dripping wet
Feeling your hands all over me is amazing

It doesn't take much for you to get me ready
My body quivers and shivers as you kiss all over my body
I am listening to you in my ears
as you caress my breast
making my tunnel wetter and wetter
Oh, won't you to take me away
to world of excess
the passion of love making
and hot sex is very amazing

Message from the Author

How many times have you felt that
no one ever love you right?
It's a few that might get it right and
learn how to love you right way.
Then there are a lot of individuals that
may never get it right because
they do not worry about what that person needs.
A lot of people are so concerned about
their happiness and self-gain. Loving
someone the right way takes
absolute trust, respect, and loving yourself fully
so you can love the other individual the right way.
When we do not love ourselves enough, we use the other
people to help ourselves feel love.
Most of the time these individuals
did not get enough love
or attention growing up,
Most of them did not feel that they were being
treated right by someone in the past,
or they were abused at some point in their life.
They felt that love from someone else could complete
the love they were missing before.
A lot of times, we want to be loved right away
when we are not completely honest with ourselves.
We lack on loving ourselves, trusting ourselves, and
respecting ourselves.
We need to use our own tools of self-love, self-worth,
and self-respect to build our self up
before we decide on getting into a relationship.

⁊

If we take these lovely steps, it'll be a lot less of people
in toxic situations and
they'll be in a committed relationship.
For your partner to love you correctly,
you must love yourself correctly.
We tend to lack the ability to treat ourselves correctly
but want others to love of correctly.
We must show people how much love
When you are showing people that you know how to
appreciate yourself,
they have no other choose but to follow.
It takes time to have the level of love for yourself to where
you do not need anyone to make you happy.
You must appreciate and love all your imperfections.
Regardless of your past, your present, and your future.
You should never let anyone discourage you from the
power you hold inside you. The key to get someone to love
you the right way is
LOVING YOURSELF THE RIGHT WAY FIRST.
WITHIN YOUR HEART AND SOUL, YOU THEN WILL BE TRULY
HAPPY.

HOW TO BE ENCOURAGED

In life we ride on such a roller coaster of event that tends
to happen and changes our view of ourselves, how we
view others, and how we view the world. Many things in
this cruel world can leave us less encouraged about
ourselves. It can be things from childhood that is ruining
the way we look at life and people. Different reasons of
certain situations can leave a bad taste in your mouths.
We have used these different situations and lessons in life
to navigate through how we stay afloat.
Use your positive moments for strength.
Use the amazing things you have accomplished to be what
inspires you to stay encouraged.
There are many ways to stay encouraged.
A lot of times, life can make you feel like
all the walls are falling.
You can use different quotes which can inspire you and
help you motivate your day and your mind.
You can use a song that motivates and inspires you about
how you feel about yourself and redirect your mind to
positive thoughts and emotions.
You should also have positive and inspiring people around
so that your energy can be shifted to happiness and peace.
Most times, it's the people that we have around us or in
our space that can be reason that we do not stay
encouraged about life, our goals and our happiness.
We must remember that staying encouraged and
remaining focus is the task at hand in your world because
the moment you lose that energy, a lot of negatives
and many clouds of judgement begin to happen. We have
stay in encourage in order to succeed at life.

Reflections Questions

When have there been a time in your life that you did not feel encouraged?

What do you do to encourage yourself?

What is some way to encourage others on their journey of life?

When was the last time you have took the time out to encourage someone else?

Take this moment to reflect on life and if your genuinely happy with the decisions you made on your journey.

Some of your decisions you might not be too happy with. Ask yourself the hard questions of where you want to be and what you want your life to be like. Many times, we just settle for what we have because we live in fear of going for your dreams. You have lack of confidence in yourself and what you can truly accomplish if you put your mind and efford to it.

I had a few times that I doubted myself when I was thinking about writing my first book. I was worried on what people might say, think or feel. I was concerned on if people were going to like what I had to say. I was concerned about talking about my struggles that I encountered.

The key to your success is to at least try to accomplish your dreams. Work hard at the goals and make the efford to carry out your dreams. The only failure you can achieve is not trying at all. The lack of determination of your dreams and wanting more for your success.

STAYING GOODBYE TO MY YESTEREDAY

Yesterday I was hurt
Today I am amazing

Yesterday I was weak
Today I was strong

Yesterday I was lonely
Today I have comforted

Yesterday I was unhappy
Today I am loved

Yesterday will always be a replay
And tomorrow will always be my future

As I forget past
I use it as my lesson for my future

Remember we fight to be better
Remember we fight to love again
Remember we fight to love all the things within
Remember you have all the power to prevail.

Yes, your yesterday was a hard road
but remember your today will help you have a
stronger future of peace and joy

How many different times have you tried
to quit on yourself?
Many times, I felt that I was not good enough to be a
writer.
I felt as if my poetry was worth reading.
A lot that was the lack of knowing that there was
power in my words.
As humans, we allow others to tell us that we
are not great at what we do or what we dream
of doing.
A lot of time, they are putting doubt in us, so we will
not be greater than them.
Most people that you think is for you, are only there
to see you to fail.
You must keep your true dreams quiet because the
person you are confiding in does not want you to
succeed. They are putting you down and giving
you lack confidence on your journey.

*REMEMBER YOUR JOURNEY IS NOT THEIR'S SO
THEY WILL NOT GIVE YOUR DREAM THAT MUCH
HELP!!*

WALKING IN YOUR TRUTH

Many times, we must truly walk in our truth because
that helps with removing the mask
that we are carrying.
So many times, we have a lack of confidence, lack
of self-esteem and lack of knowledge of self-
worth for ourselves

We must walk in your truth in order to acknowledge
all the true things about yourself that we do
not enjoy others to knowing

Many times, we put mask on because we had a hard
childhood life, you were abused,
or felt like you were not fitting in.
Most of us lived in fear of judgement,
we feel as if people do not understand
your struggles and who you really are.

We must learn to remove the mask to be able to
walk in our truth.
You must truly embrace the imperfections
and absolutely love the internal to the bottom of
your soul to be able to walk in your truth

Many people lack the power to absolutely
love themselves because of things
that have been said to them,
they way you view yourself, and lack of love
and attention they endure through years

A lot times, we have passed down the failures of
others generations before us because they did
not give you the tools to love
who you are behind your mask.
We must sometimes become self-taught and
reconstruct the things that we have learned from
generations before us because of the
damage it has done to us

I learned to walk in my truth and in the past few
months, I had to allowed my mask
to be let down in order to heal.
I was determined to not let my next
generation repeat the same pattern
that was before me.
Teaching them the tools of knowledge of who
they are, how to love themselves, and knowledge of
self-worth.

It is an honor to have your kids tell you that they
want to be just like you, and you are their hero.
It is an honor to hear your children
say they are proud of me.
I step out of the shadow and made a lane
for my kids to walk in.
I gave them the vison of the things they can do
if they walk in their truth.

I had people tell me that I couldn't be a writer and
my books are never going to go anywhere. You may
also have people who are going to count

you out but just remember to have

determination and ambition.
I still had faith in myself. I was strong enough to
reach for the stars even over the hard road.

Many people do not know how to move on from
the obstacles in life. We sometime are so stuck that you

feel as if you cannot get out of the rut that you are in. We all been in different barriers in our lifetimes that we need to overcome. Stop letting that be your enemy.

I have had many obstacles that have I felt as if I could not get over. I have three different health conditions that I do not allow to stop me from being the best version of myself. I also do not allow anyone to persuade my dream.

When I think of the topics of overcoming your barriers so many different things come to mind. We have so many different things that can be a barrier that can get in your way as obstacles. There are many things that is or can be a stumbling block or interruption. Some people have dealt with racism, discrimination, and violence, just to name a few.

I am single mother on welfare. I am a survivor of domestic violence, and I also have a chronic illness that I deal with on a daily basis. I have also dealt with my own racism, discrimination, and violence at different points in my life.

Dealing with the different barriers can be a hinder to you at some point in your journey of life. Just do not let it be a struggling barrier that cannot overcome to get through life. Overcoming barriers is like winning your power back in life. Regaining the freedom that they have taken from you when you know that you should be free.

My first barrier I had to overcome was being on welfare. No not saying that there is anything wrong with being on

welfare but I feel that since I have a BA degree in Sociology, I paid too much money for this degree to be stuck here with not enough money to take care of my two kids. I am working minimum wage jobs making ends meet.
You must work hard to fix your situations.

My next situation is now being abuses by someone I thought loved me. Which left me broken, ashamed, depress, and struggling with two kids. My options were either stay in that position or do something to make it better. I choose to elevate myself from barriers that was sitting as a stumbling block.

In the mission to living in a better world, the world threw a few rocks in my path. Now I was faced with not being able to work a 9 to 5 job because my body is fighting against me. My condition became a roadblock. I was not having it. I struggled for years a trying to figuring out what was wrong. Once again, depression start setting in. I felt like a failure and did not help that I was in as second domestic violence situation.

When dealing with those barriers, you then turn to yourself and ask the question "How am I going affect change my situations?"
The moment you let doubt settle in, that's when you set yourself up to not be successful. We must remember that there are people that already want to see you fail. When they already discriminated against you, you already deal or dealt with racism, or being through violence they are already counting us out.

We must stand tall and be present for what we stand for. As I work on overcoming my barriers, I had to remember who I am. What I was all about. What I was taught, and how I was raised to be strong, powerful, ambitious, and ready to conquer the world.

I started to empower myself through my spiritual growth and working on my poetry, and I believed in myself. Remember that I must believe in myself in order to do better in life. My children became my reasoning of why I had not let myself not be a product of my environment. I could not let my barriers be the reason why I did not overcome my situations. My goals and vision are to see my children do better than me.

I encourage you to remain powerful, regardless of how many times the world throws you a barrier at you to overcome. Always remember to remain focused and know that your power comes from within you. Remember you have the power to help bring change to this world one strives at a time. Help people in society to understand that we can have difference of opinions, but we are all equal. Stand strong for your truth and true purpose of what you are here for.

Shana W. Gourdine

About the Author

I am from the big city of Cross SC, born in November 23, 1980 in Charleston, South Carolina. I received my B.A. in Sociology from Morris College, Sumter SC. I have my life coaching certification and culinary arts certification as well. I am a mother of two beautiful daughters, Leonna and Samira, which are my pride and joy. During this journey of transparency, I learned that you can survive through all things as long as you fight through it. You have to know where your power lives within you. I learned to trust my gut feelings and thoughts to pursure my dreams. I will continue this journey of helping people learn their true self regardless of their imperfections; despite their story. I am here to use my scars as healing for others and I will continue to be a vessel of healing.

After reading this book, how do you feel?

_____

_____

_____

_____

_____

_____

_____

_____

_____

_____

What pieces of a broken mask are you proud to let go of?

_____

What steps will you take to get out of your current situation?

Use this space to Journal your thoughts

_____

_____

_____

_____

_____

_____

List positive affirmations about yourself

_____

_____

_____

_____

_____

_____

_____

_____

_____

_____

Journal your thoughts

_____

_____

_____

_____

_____

_____

_____

_____

_____

_____

_____

Know your self worth. Share one thing that you love about yourself.

_____

_____

_____

_____

_____

_____

_____

_____

_____

_____

Share your goals, dreams and your thoughts.

_____

_____

_____

_____

_____

_____

_____

_____

_____

_____

_____

_____

_____

_____

_____

_____

_____

_____

_____

_____

_____

_____

_____

_____

_____

_____

_____

_____

_____

_____

_____

_____

_____

_____

_____

_____

_____

_____

_____

_____

_____

_____

_____

_____

_____

_____

_____

_____

_____

_____

_____

_____

_____

_____

_____

_____

_____

_____

_____

_____

_____

_____

_____

_____

_____

_____

_____

_____

_____

_____

_____

_____

_____

_____

_____

_____

_____

_____

_____

_____

_____

_____

_____

_____

_____

_____

_____

_____

_____

_____

_____

_____

_____